40 Fabulous Social Studies Activities

by Catherine M. Tamblyn

NEW YORK ● TORONTO ● LONDON ● AUCKLAND ● SYDNEY
MEXICO CITY ● NEW DELHI ● HONG KONG ● BUENOS AIRES

Teaching Resources

To family and friends, inclusive of the little ones,

to teens, who amuse and amaze me daily

and offer joy and laughter as they travel my path

and include me on theirs.

Edited by Immacula Rhodes
Cover design by Scott Davis
Interior design by Kathy Massaro
Interior illustrations by Kate Flanagan

ISBN 978-0-545-31505-0

1 2 3 4 5 6 7 8 9 10   40   20 19 18 17 16 15 14 13

Contents

Introduction

Welcome to *40 Fabulous Social Studies Activities*! This unique collection of flexible, easy-to-make projects provides students with engaging and meaningful ways to prepare, present, and display what they learn about a wide range of social studies topics.

Each project links to one or more areas of study—geography, map skills, places, time, history, people, citizenship, environment, government, economics, and celebrations—and can be used to extend and enhance your primary social studies curriculum. Students follow easy, step-by-step directions to create the projects using information they have learned through research and reading. Activities encourage students to apply steps related to the research and writing processes, such as choosing a topic, planning, researching (locating resources, reading, taking notes), outlining and writing, revising, editing, and publishing or producing the final product. The varied and flexible nature of the projects appeals to students of all learning styles and helps make Social Studies exciting and fun.

The projects in this resource—collages, dioramas, banners, scrolls, quilts, hangers, a variety of book formats, and much more—require little preparation. Most materials are available in the classroom or can be gathered with relative ease. In fact, recyclable or reusable items make ideal materials for many of the activities. Also, you may need to make available tools, such as a calendar, globe, atlas, United States and World wall maps, student outline maps, and a compass, for student reference in preparing or presenting their projects.

Whether you want to introduce new topics, reinforce previously learned information, or expand students' knowledge, these projects provide a meaningful way to reinforce learning while building reading, writing, and research skills. The activities also help support you in meeting national standards for Social Studies and Language Arts (see page 8).

To get started, choose the project of your choice from the Contents (page 3) or check the Topic Matrix (page 7) to find projects that work well for the area of study you have in mind. But don't limit yourself to the suggestions on the matrix—keep in mind that many of the activities can be used for most any topic or area of study. So be flexible and creative when matching up projects to topics. Then enjoy the fun to come!

About This Book

What's Inside

The projects in this book can be easily integrated into your curriculum and used at any time of the year. For each project, you'll find information that includes the following:

- **Introduction:** This text gives a brief description of the project and its use.

- **Materials:** Check this section to find a list of materials students need to make the project. For most, basic classroom supplies—such as paper, markers or crayons, scissors, and glue—are all that are needed. Additional items, such as cardboard tubes, craft sticks, and recyclable materials are included in the list where applicable. The reproducible pattern pages listed for some activities make your preparation time minimal.

- **Step-by-Step Directions:** These easy-to-follow directions explain how to make the project. For some activities, you'll find alternative suggestions for assembling the project.

- **Tips:** This section offers helpful suggestions for preparing, making, and using the project.

- **Content Connection:** This activity suggests how to prepare the project to feature or reinforce a particular topic or concept. If a reproducible pattern is needed to complete the project, you'll find it on the page following this section. Students can create the project as described, or you might adapt the activity to meet their needs or interests.

- **Other Content Connections:** The list in this section suggests other topics that work well with the project. In addition to these topics, you'll most likely come up with many more of your own. Be open-minded and creative—the flexible format of the projects offers a broad range of possibilities for featuring topics and concepts. Note that for Versatile Cubes (page 10), you'll find a list of variations for labeling and using the cube.

Management Tips

- Prepare each project in advance to become familiar with the materials and directions. (You might make the project described in Content Connection.)

- Before students begin to make their project, have them do research, plan, and write drafts of the text they will include in the project. Making the project will be the last step of their research and writing process.

- In advance, gather and prepare all materials needed to make the project. Many projects use materials you already have in your classroom. Recyclable items may be listed for some projects, and you may choose to use recyclables wherever possible for others. See Recycle and Reuse! (below) for suggested items that you might collect and have available when ready to make projects.

- Review the materials and directions with students. Demonstrate how to make each project before they make their own. If desired, use your completed sample as a model for students to refer to as they work on their projects.

- Feel free to modify or customize the projects in any way desired to meet your students' specific needs or interests.

- Invite students to share their projects with the class and discuss what they have learned about the topic featured on their project.

- Prepare displays to feature students' projects. Consider showcasing their work in the hallways, media center, or school display cases.

Recycle and Reuse!

Many of the recyclable items below can be used in a number of the projects. You might thumb through the pages of this resource to identify projects that use recyclables or include materials that could be replaced with recyclable items. Make a list, then start collecting so the items will be on hand when you're ready to introduce the projects to students.

cardboard	junk mail envelopes	refrigerator or appliance boxes
cardboard tubes	large plastic lids	scrap paper
catalogs and magazines	newspapers	shoeboxes
egg cartons	plastic berry baskets	shredded paper
foam packing peanuts	plastic containers	travel guides and brochures
foam trays	plastic soda bottles	wallpaper
gift wrap	oatmeal and chip canisters	wire shirt hangers

Topic Matrix

Activity	Geography	Map Skills	Places	Time	History	People	Citizenship	Environment	Government	Economics	Celebrations
Paper-Bag Sleeve Books	*	*	*								
Versatile Cubes	*	*	*								
Collaborative Collages	*	*	*			*		*	*		
Box Dioramas	*		*		*			*			
Circle Compasses	*	*	*								
Sack Structures		*	*		*	*					
Pocket-Folder Suitcases	*	*	*					*			
Starry Facts Chains	*	*	*		*						*
Band Books	*	*	*		*	*	*		*		
Pocket Books	*	*	*		*	*		*			
Stack-and-Fold Books	*	*	*		*				*		
Time Capsules			*	*	*	*		*			
Timeline Event Hangers			*	*	*	*		*	*	*	*
Biography Hanger Frames					*	*	*				*
Birthday Marker Hangers				*	*	*					*
Trading Cards		*	*	*	*	*					
Cut-Away Books				*	*	*	*		*		*
Wrap-Around Monuments				*	*	*			*		
Portrait Plates				*	*	*			*		
Simple Shutter Books	*			*	*	*			*		
Shutter House Books			*	*	*	*					
Mix-and-Match Flip Books			*	*	*	*			*		
Facts-on-Flaps Booklets	*		*	*	*	*			*		
Supersize Stamps				*	*	*					
Codex Books	*		*	*	*	*			*		
Trifold Table Toppers			*	*	*	*			*		
Portable Partitions				*	*	*		*	*		*
Banner Hang-Ups						*	*	*	*		
Class Scrolls						*	*		*		
Poster-Board Shields					*	*	*		*		*
Theme Quilts			*	*	*	*			*		
Folding Fans			*		*		*	*			*
One-Cut Pennants							*	*		*	
3-D Flow Charts				*				*		*	
Recyclables Frames						*	*	*		*	*
Accordion Shape Books				*	*	*	*			*	*
Stage Triforms	*		*	*	*	*			*		
Quadruple Triforms				*	*	*				*	*
Zip Books	*	*	*					*		*	*
Folding Postcards	*	*	*		*	*	*				

40 Fabulous Social Studies Activities © 2013 by Catherine M. Tamblyn, Scholastic Teaching Resources

Connections to the Standards

The activities in this book are designed to support you in meeting the following standards for students in grades 2–3, as outlined by Mid-continent Research for Education and Learning (McREL), an organization that collects and synthesizes national and state K–12 curriculum standards.

History

- Understands family life now and in the past, and family life in various places long ago

- Understands how democratic values came to be, and how they have been exemplified by people, events, and symbols

- Understands the causes and nature of movements of large groups of people into and within the United States, now and long ago

- Understands major discoveries in science and technology, some of their social and economic effects, and the major scientist and inventors responsible for them

Civics

- Understands ideas about civic life, politics, and government

- Understands the sources, purposes, and functions of law, and the importance of the rule of law for the protection of individual rights and the common good

- Understands the role of diversity in American life and the importance of shared values, political beliefs, and civic beliefs in an increasingly diverse American society

- Understands issues concerning the relationship between state and local governments and the national government and issues pertaining to representation at all three levels of government

- Understands the meaning of citizenship in the United States

Geography

- Understands the characteristics and uses of maps, globes, and other geographic tools and technologies

- Knows the location of places, geographic features, and patterns of the environment

- Understands the characteristics of ecosystems on Earth's surface

- Understands the patterns and networks of economic interdependence on Earth's surface

- Understands how human actions modify the physical environment

- Understands the changes that occur in the meaning, use, distribution, and importance of resources

Source: Kendall, J. S., & Marzano, R. J. (2004). *Content knowledge: A compendium of standards and benchmarks for K–12 education*. Aurora, CO: Mid-continent Research for Education and Learning. Online database: http://www.mcrel.org/standards-benchmarks/

The activities in this book also align with the Writing Standards for English Language Arts as outlined by the Common Core State Standards Initiative (CCSSI) for grades 2–3. For more information, visit the CCSSI website at www.corestandards.org.

Writing

Text Types and Purposes

- W.2.2. Write informative/explanatory texts in which they introduce a topic, use facts and definitions to develop points, and provide a concluding statement or section.

- W.3.2, W.3.2a, W.3.2b. Write informative/explanatory texts to examine a topic and convey ideas and information clearly.

Production and Distribution of Writing

- W.2.5. With guidance and support from adults and peers, focus on a topic and strengthen writing as needed by revising and editing.

- W.3.4. With guidance and support from adults, produce writing in which the development and organization are appropriate to task and purpose.

Research to Build and Present Knowledge

- W.2.7. Participate in shared research and writing projects (e.g., read a number of books on a single topic to produce a report; record science observations).

- W.3.7. Conduct short research projects that build knowledge about a topic.

Paper-Bag Sleeve Books

Sleeve books, created with new or gently used paper lunch bags, are ideal for helping students organize note cards, vocabulary words, facts, and pictures on any social studies topic.

Materials

For each student:

- ruler
- paper lunch bags
- hole punch
- 12-inch length of ribbon or yarn
- 3- by 5-inch index cards

Tips

- Students can add pages as they learn more about their topic.
- Students might make books with large paper bags to organize or store class work, oversized maps, and components of ongoing projects.

Other Content Connections

- U.S. regions and states
- state and national parks
- continents and oceans

1 Punch two holes about 3 inches apart through the bottom of one bag.

2 Use this bag as a guide to punch matching holes in additional bags. (The number of bags will vary depending on how many pages are needed for the book).

3 Stack the bags, bottom flap down, and align the holes.

4 Bind the bags together with ribbon or yarn.

Content Connection: Geography Words

Provide students with a list of geography words, a lunch bag for each listed word plus an extra bag to use as a cover, and plain index cards. First, students make a sleeve book. Then they design the cover, label each sleeve (bag) with a word from the list, and add illustrations, if desired. For each listed word, students create cards labeled with the definition, illustrations, or other information that describes the word. For example, they can define, illustrate, or describe physical characteristics of a particular body of water, as well as include a map with symbols indicating its location. Finally, students insert the word list into the cover sleeve (for use as a table of contents) and each card into the corresponding word sleeve.

Versatile Cubes

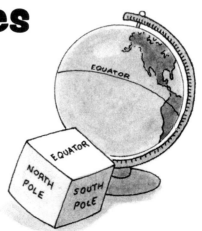

Three-dimensional cubes provide a flexible format on which students can record a variety of information, including map-related vocabulary, map symbols, capital cities, countries, continents, and small illustrations of geographical features.

Materials

For each cube:
- cube pattern (page 11)
- scissors
- pencil, markers, or crayons
- glue stick

1 Cut out the cube pattern.

2 Label or illustrate the faces of the cube.

3 Fold along the lines, as shown.

4 Glue the tabs in place.

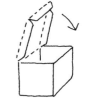

Tips
- You might copy the cube pattern onto sturdy paper, such as construction paper or tagboard.
- If you plan to make a cube for repeated group use, laminate it for durability.

Content Connection: Global Toss-and-Find

Students label each side of their cube cutout with the name of a place (such as a country, capital city, or continent), geographic feature (for example, a specific landform or body of water), or a feature on a globe (such as the Equator, North Pole, South Pole, or a specific latitude or longitude). After assembling their cubes, students place them in a large paper bag. Then they take turns drawing a cube from the bag, tossing it, and naming the item it lands on. Finally, they locate that item on a map or globe.

Variations

For variations of Global Toss-and-Find, label the cube with the following and use with the suggested props:

Cube Labels	Additional Props
state names or abbreviations	U.S. map
state capitals	political map
map symbols	landform map

40 Fabulous Social Studies Activities © 2013 by Catherine M. Tamblyn, Scholastic Teaching Resources

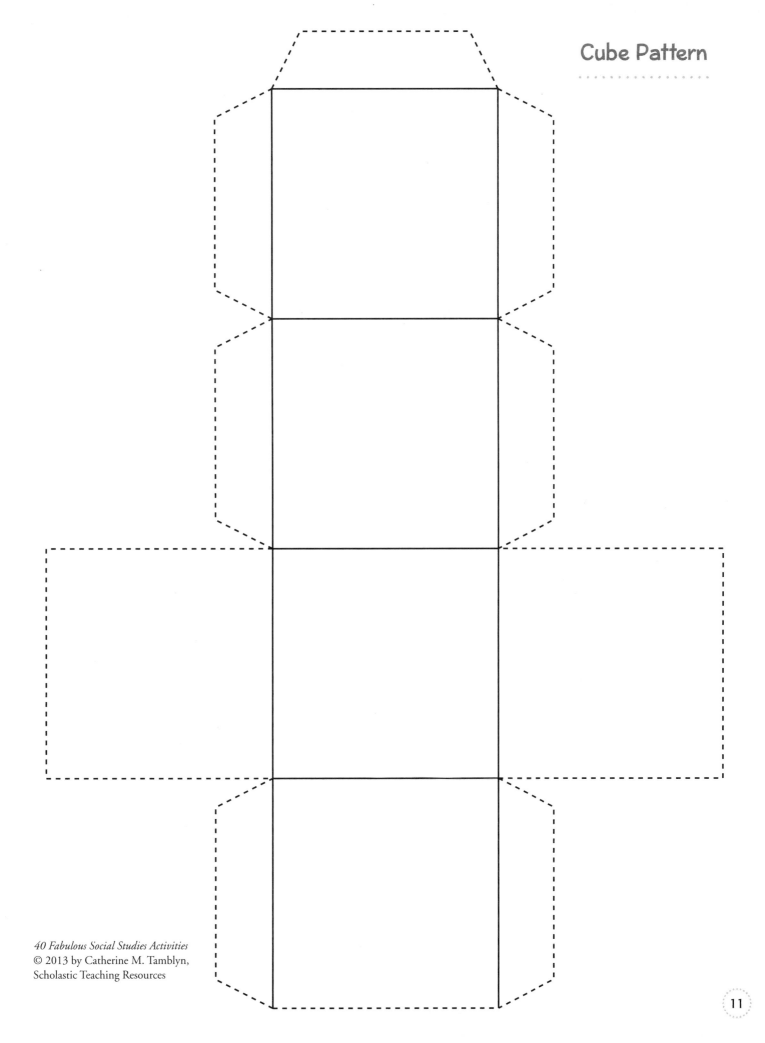

Collaborative Collages

Collages make great group projects that involve all students in locating, sorting, cutting, arranging, and gluing art and text to assimilate and summarize what they have learned about a particular topic.

Materials

For each student or group:

- large sheet of drawing paper or tagboard
- recycled newspapers, magazines, catalogs, travel guides, and brochures
- scissors
- glue sticks

Tips

- Use clothespins or metal binder clips to hang the collages from a clothesline.
- Students might create individual self-standing collages by gluing picture and text cutouts to the inside of file folders.

Other Content Connections

- local places (school, park, supermarket) and workers
- habitats or ecosystems
- local, state, or regional resources

1 Find and cut out pictures and words that relate to an assigned theme. Or, prepare art and text related to the theme.

2 Glue the cutouts onto drawing paper or tagboard. Place the cutouts in an interesting arrangement, overlapping and positioning them at angles, and so on.

3 Add a title to the collage.

Content Connection: Community Themes

Small groups of students create collages on assigned communities, such as rural, suburban, and urban communities. As they gather images and text, group members discuss the components they gather to ensure that each one relates to their topic. Once all the components are collected, group members work together to arrange and glue them to the background paper.

To extend, use removable tape to make a coordinate grid on the theme collage. Affix numbered sticky notes along the top of the grid to label the columns. Add lettered sticky notes along the left side to label the rows. Students use the grid to identify the coordinates that mark the location of a specific item, such as the square that contains a skating rink.

40 Fabulous Social Studies Activities © 2013 by Catherine M. Tamblyn, Scholastic Teaching Resources

Box Dioramas

Students can create dioramas—miniature, lifelike representations of a community, historical site, landform, or other scene—from boxes of various sizes and shapes.

The town square is the best part of my town, Ridgewood. It is my favorite place because there is a fun playground and a big fountain to toss in pennies and make wishes. by Hailey Franco

Materials

For each student or group:

- empty box, such as a cereal, cracker, or shirt box
- pencil
- ruler
- craft knife (optional: for adult use only)
- markers (or crayons)
- assorted craft materials
- scissors
- glue

Tip

In advance, students might paint their box a solid color.

Other Content Connections

- types of communities (past and present)
- U.S. and global environments
- historical or natural landmarks

1 Draw a large, rectangular flap on the face of the box. Use a long edge of the box as the bottom side of the flap. (This edge will form the hinge for the flap.) Leave a one-inch border around the other three sides of the flap.

2 Cut out the flap along the side and top lines, as shown. (Do not cut the bottom edge.)

3 Stand the box on the long end, open the flap, and flatten to extend the box floor.

4 Use markers and craft materials to decorate the inside (and outside) of the box.

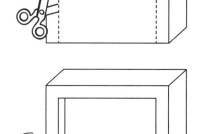

Content Connections: My Community

Students construct a diorama that depicts a special place in their own community, such as a town square, park, or library. They can use their own illustrations, magazine cutouts, or craft supplies to design structures and objects for their diorama. Students might glue items directly to the base or sides of the diorama. They can add 3-D characteristics to other items by standing them upright in small lumps of clay or attaching them to accordion-folded paper strips, or "springs." To add information about their scenes, students might write (or glue) descriptive text to the flap of their diorama.

Circle Compasses

Materials

For each student
or group:

- compass rose
  pattern (page 15)
- markers
- scissors
- 9-inch paper plate
- glue
- hole punch
- 36-inch length
  of yarn

Circle compasses are simple to make and easy for students to tote to any destination in which you want to reinforce directions.

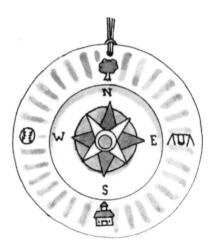

1 Color and cut out the compass rose. Glue the cutout to the center of the plate.

2 Punch a hole in the plate above N (for North).

3 For the hanger, knot the yarn ends together. Thread the looped end of the yarn (opposite the knot) through the hole. Then slide the knotted end through the loop and pull to secure.

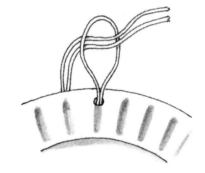

4 The compass can be worn as a necklace when moving from place to place.

Tip

To find true North without a compass, students go outdoors at midday and stand with their shadows directly in front of them. (The shadow off the top of their head will point north.) A partner draws a chalk arrow on pavement pointing North for use as a reference. (Caution students not to look directly at the sun.)

Other Content Connections

Students can use the following to find symbols, pictures, or places to represent on their compass:

- U.S. or state maps
- community map
- world map or globe

Content Connection: Compass Caper

After students make their circle compass, take small groups to different settings around the school, such as the playground, cafeteria, and media center. In that location, students face true North. (Use a real compass.) Then they locate a landmark, structure, or object for each direction on their compass (N, S, E, and W) and draw a symbol to represent that item on their compass. Students should choose objects that are stationary. For example, on a playground setting, a student might draw a tree above N on their compass, a swing set next to E, a school below S, and a baseball (for a ballfield) beside W. Later, students can exchange compasses, use the symbols to identify the mystery location, then visit that location to find the objects represented on the compass.

40 Fabulous Social Studies Activities © 2013 by Catherine M. Tamblyn, Scholastic Teaching Resources

Compass Rose Pattern

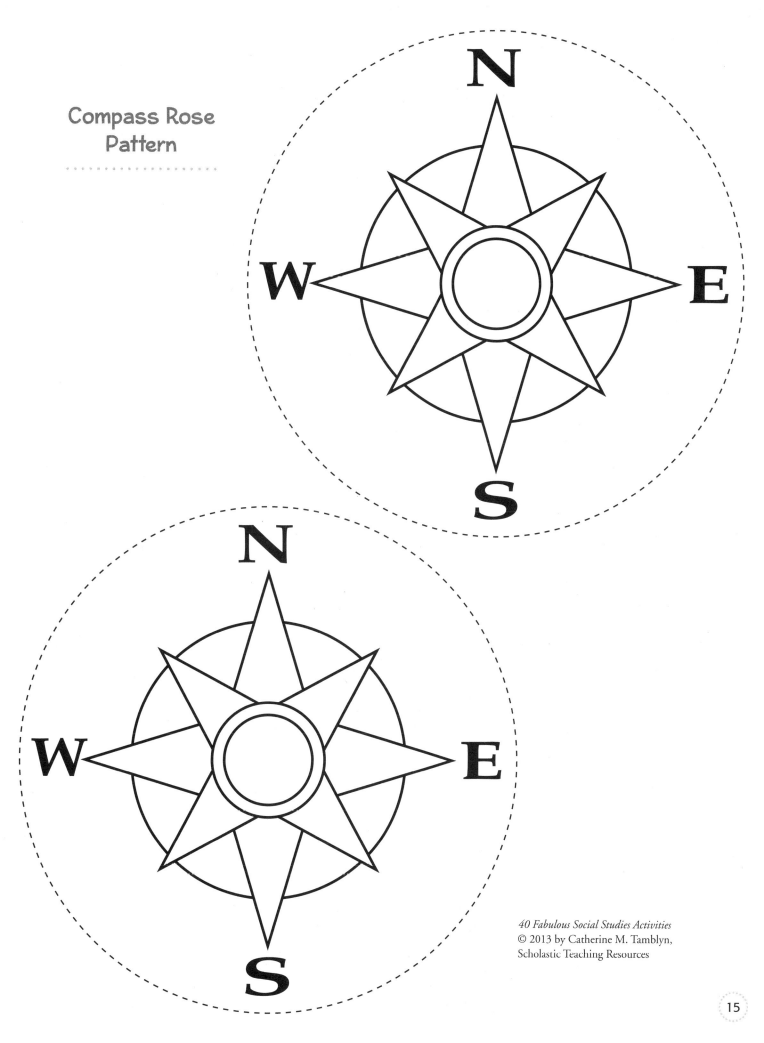

40 Fabulous Social Studies Activities
© 2013 by Catherine M. Tamblyn,
Scholastic Teaching Resources

Sack Structures

Sack structures made from plain paper lunch bags and assorted craft items give students a creative way to construct models of buildings, neighborhoods, and communities.

Make a Single Sack Structure

(requires one paper bag)

1 Place a paper bag vertically with the opening at the top. Decorate the bag to represent the structure of choice, such as a house or store. Leave space at the top to fold down the bag and form a roof (see step 3).

2 Stand the bag upright and fill it halfway with the stuffing material.

3 Fold down and glue (or staple) the top of the bag in place to form the desired roof style, as follows:

POINTED ROOF: fold back the two top corners together until they meet in the middle.

FLAT ROOF: fold down the entire top part of the bag about two inches.

4 Add trimmings and finishing details to the structure.

Make a Tall Sack Structure

(requires two paper bags)

1 Place one paper bag vertically with the bottom flap at the top. Decorate the bag to represent a tall building, such as a skyscraper. (The bottom flap will be the roof.)

2 Stand the other bag upright and fill it with stuffing.

3 Slip the decorated bag over the stuffed bag.

4 Decorate the two narrow sides of the structure. Add trimmings and other finishing details.

Make a Horizontal Sack Structure
(requires two paper bags)

1 Place one paper bag horizontally and decorate it to represent a short, wide building, such as single-story school. One narrow side of the bag will be the roof.

2 Open the other bag and fill it with stuffing.

3 Fit the stuffed bag, open end first, into the decorated bag.

4 Stand the structure upright. (The bottom of each bag will be a side wall of the building.) Decorate the sides of the structure. Add trimmings and other finishing details.

Content Connection: Sack-Structure Communities

Students work in small groups to plan a community and decide which sack-structure styles to use for the buildings. They might create structures to represent buildings in a colonial settlement, suburban neighborhood, or Pueblo village. (Note that students can stack and glue horizontal structures together to create wide, multi-level buildings.) To complete their communities, students can create models of objects (flags, fountains, or fire pits), natural features (trees), and people to add to their scene. Finally, groups can use their models in presentations about life in that community, including identifying the buildings by their functions (such as homes, stores, and community services).

Other Content Connections

- famous homes (White House, Mount Vernon, Lincoln's log cabin)
- historic settlements (Plymouth, Jamestown)
- neighborhoods and communities (urban, suburban, rural)

Pocket-Folder Suitcases

These unique suitcases are ideal for storing reports, or to fill with interesting facts, mementos, and maps of places students "visit" in their studies.

Materials

For each student:
- 9-inch paper plate
- scissors
- two-pocket folder with paper fasteners
- glue stick
- two $\frac{1}{2}$-inch self-adhesive Velcro® dots (optional)
- markers and other decorating supplies

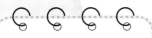

Other Content Connections

- the U.S. or other country
- states (past or present)
- continents and oceans

1 Cut out the inner part of the paper plate, leaving a one-inch wide rim. Cut the rim in two (for suitcase handles).

2 Open the folder (suitcase) and glue a handle to the inside edge of one side. Glue the second handle to the opposite side, matching the placement of the first handle.

3 For fasteners, affix a Velcro® dot to the suitcase on either side of each handle. (Use the loop dots on one side of the suitcase and the hook dots on the other side.) Check that the dots match up when the suitcase is closed.

4 Close and fasten the suitcase. Decorate the front and back to represent the chosen theme for the suitcase.

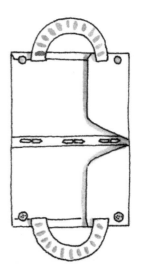

Content Connection: My Travels

Students make a suitcase to hold a collection of maps and other items related to places they have visited or would like to visit. To add materials (such as maps and fliers) to their suitcase, students can punch three holes along one edge of each item, aligning the holes with the paper fasteners in their suitcase. They can then fasten the item inside the folder. Similarly, they might punch holes in clasp envelopes or resealable plastic bags to create closeable pockets for storing odd-sized or smaller items, such as brochures, fact cards, postcards, pictures, and souvenirs.

Starry Facts Chains

These chains are a celestial way to display the "star attractions" of a state, region, local community, or country.

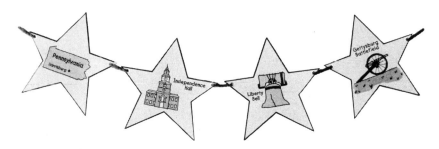

1 Cut out the tagboard star to use as a template.

2 Trace the template onto construction paper and cut it out. Repeat, making as many stars as desired.

3 Decorate one or both sides of each star with drawings, picture cutouts, text, maps, or other items related to the chosen topic.

4 To make a horizontal chain, punch a hole in the left and right points of each star. For a vertical chain, punch a hole at the top point and base of each star.

5 Connect the stars using paper clips, as shown (see above and at right).

6 Attach yarn to the first and last star in the horizontal chain to serve as hangers. Tie yarn to the top star to make a hanger for the vertical chain.

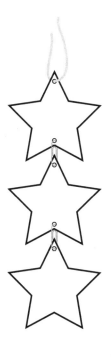

Other Content Connections

- communities
- countries
- holiday traditions and customs of various countries

Content Connection: State Star Attractions

Students choose a state and research the special attractions in that state, such national parks, historical sites, monuments, and natural wonders. They decide which attractions to feature on a starry fact chain and cut out the appropriate number of stars. On the first star, they glue on or draw an outline of their state and label it with the state name. Then they decorate a star for each attraction, writing facts and interesting information about the attraction on the back. To display, suspend students' chains around the room. To extend the activity, students can find the location of their state and featured attractions on a large U.S. map.

Star Pattern

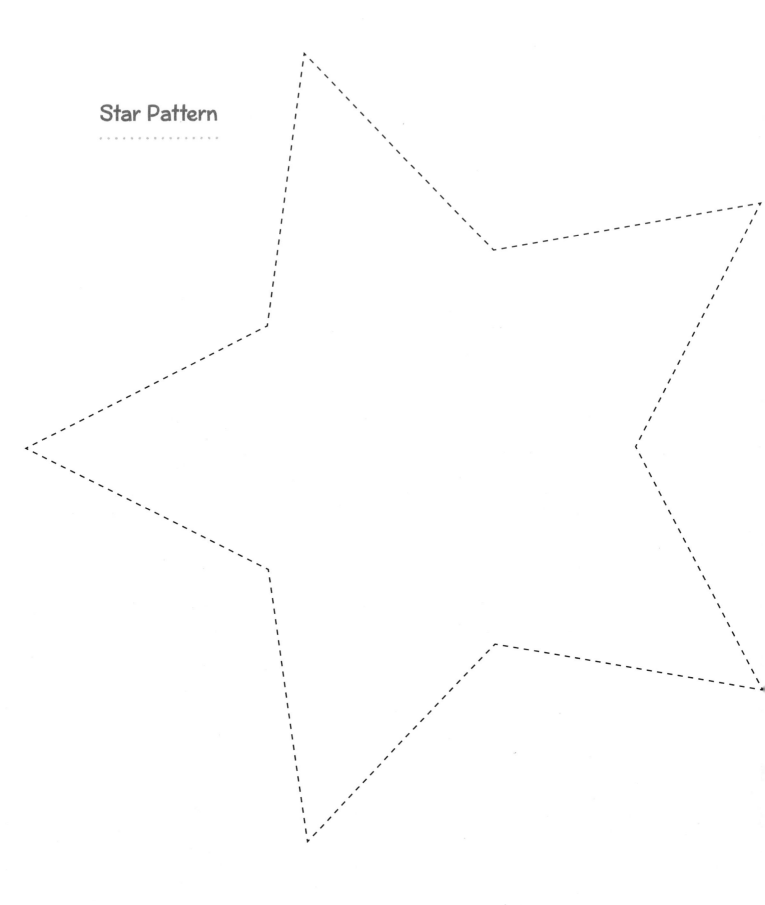

Band Books

The rubber-band handles of these easy-to-make, compact band books allow students to keep them handy by wearing the books on their wrists.

For each student:
- $8\frac{1}{2}$ - by 11-inch copy paper
- scissors
- long rubber band (about 7 inches in length)

Tips

- Students can design a cover for their book and use the front and back of each interior page to add art and record information about their topic.

- To make a book with fewer pages, use one sheet of $8\frac{1}{2}$ - by 11-inch paper.

Other Content Connections

- market products and country of origin
- inventors, inventions, and their birthplaces
- historical American leaders

1 For a book with eight pages, stack and fold two sheets of paper in half the long way.

2 Cut along the fold through both layers to make four strips of paper.

3 Stack the strips, then fold in half the short way.

4 Cut off both corners at an angle on the folded edge. Leave about two inches intact along the fold.

5 Unfold the pages. Wrap a rubber band twice around them at the fold line, then refold the pages.

6 Use the rubber band as a book handle or bracelet.

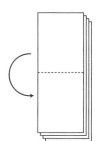

Content Connections: State Facts and Symbols

Students create a band book to fill with state-related facts and art. They can decorate the cover to represent their state, then complete the interior pages with drawings of the state map and capital, state symbols (such as the state flag, flower, bird, tree, seal, and motto), and historical figures and landmarks. Students can plan two-page spreads for each entry by drawing art on one page and adding a label or description for that art on the opposite page.

Pocket Books

Pocket book pages are fashioned with envelopes and provide an excellent question-and-answer format for students to practice topic-related facts.

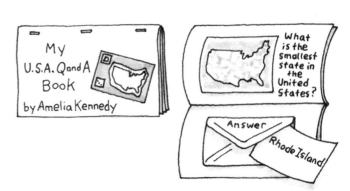

Tip

If desired, students can cover the stapled edge of their book with masking tape.

Other Content Connections

- inventors and scientists
- historical American leaders
- meaning of signs and symbols

1 Stack the desired number of sheets of paper and fold in half the short way. (Each sheet will make two pages.)

2 Staple the pages together along the folded edge.

3 Open the cover and glue an envelope, flap side up, on the lower page of the spread, as shown. Write "Answer" on the envelope. Repeat for each lower page of a spread.

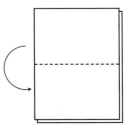

Content Connection: U.S.A. Q and A Books

Provide pencils, crayons, markers, and small copies of a United States map. Students make their pocket book and title it "My U.S.A. Q and A Book." Then they color and cut out the small map and glue it to the cover. (Or, they draw their own map.) Next, students open the cover and write a map-related question on each upper page opposite the envelope, for instance, "What is the smallest state in the United States?" They can also add a drawing or a picture to that page. Then they write the answer on the inside of the envelope flap on that spread. Or, they might write the answer on a slip of paper or index card to put inside the envelope. To use, students switch pocket books with classmates, read and answer the questions, then look inside the pockets to check their answers.

Stack-and-Fold Books

Stack-and-fold books are about the size of a passport and can be used for recording facts, writing a mini book report, taking notes, and more.

1 Stack and fold two sheets of paper in half the short way.

2 Cut along the fold through both layers to make four strips of paper.

3 Stack the strips, then fold in half the short way.

4 Staple the pages together along the fold. (The book will have eight leaves.)

5 Choose a topic to feature in the book. Decorate the cover. Add art and text to the front and back of each interior page.

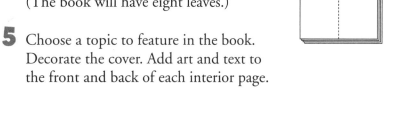

Materials

For each student:
- $8\frac{1}{2}$ - by 11-inch copy paper
- scissors
- stapler

Tip

To make a book with more pages, use additional sheets of paper. Each page will add four more pages.

Other Content Connections

- map skills (symbols, latitudes and longitudes to locate places)
- careers and occupations
- state products and resources

Content Connections: Reading Passports

Provide each student with a copy of the passport pattern on page 24. Students make a stack-and-fold book, then color, cut out, and glue their pattern to the cover. On the first spread of their book, students draw a self-portrait, or attach a small photo and record their personal information (name, birthdate, birthplace, and home country).

Students use their reading passports to record the global connections they make through literature. After reading a book that has a setting outside of the United States, they create an entry for the book in their passport on a two-page spread. To do this, students record the title, author, and location of the story and add setting-related drawings, including an outline map of the country in which the story is set. After completing each entry, students can submit it to you to be "rubber stamped" for approval.

It Takes a Village by Jane Cowen Fletcher
Setting: Benin
AFRICA
Benin

MY READING PASSPORT

by _____

MY READING PASSPORT

by _____

MY READING PASSPORT

by _____

MY READING PASSPORT

by _____

40 Fabulous Social Studies Activities © 2013 by Catherine M. Tamblyn, Scholastic Teaching Resources

Timeline Event Hangers

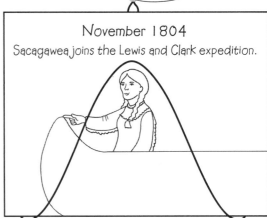

November 1804
Sacagawea joins the Lewis and Clark expedition.

Materials

For each student:
- wire shirt hanger
- pipe cleaner
- drawing paper
- crayons, markers, or colored pencils
- clothesline

Tips

- To personalize their hanger, students can wrap masking tape around the neck to make a flag, then label it with their name.

- To make dividers for the timeline, see "Tips" on page 29 and label them with the year, historical period, or topic.

Other Content Connections

- voyage of the *Mayflower*
- westward expansion
- admission of states to the U.S.A.

Timeline event hangers give students a flexible and visual way to portray the sequence of important historical events.

1 Starting at the tip of the hanger hook, coil a pipe cleaner around the hook to the neck of the hanger.

2 Bend the arms of a hanger, as shown.

3 Draw a picture of a selected historical event on paper. Label the event and add a date.

4 Slip the picture into the hanger holder, as shown above. (The picture can be placed horizontally or vertically.)

5 Add the event hanger to a clothesline timeline, placing it in its chronological position among other hangers that picture related events.

Content Connections: U.S.A. Explorations

Students prepare their hanger following steps 1 and 2 in the directions (above). Then they work in groups to research events related to an exploration of the United States, such as the Lewis and Clark expedition, creating a timeline of important events. Next, students label a page with the date and description of each event in the timeline, draw a picture of that event, and insert the page into an event hanger. For example, a group might make separate event hangers for the date Lewis and Clark began their expedition, their first Fourth of July celebration, the first sighting of animals unknown to them, the addition of Sacagawea to their party, and so on. Finally, the groups sequence their hangers on a clothesline.

Martin Luther King, Jr.
1929-1968
• Civil rights leader of the 1950's and 1960's
• Believed in equal rights for all people
• Gave his famous "I have a dream" speech in Washington, D.C.
• Holiday in his memory is in January

Biography Hanger Frames

Biography hanger frames, made from wire shirt hangers, offer a unique way for students to share and display information about national leaders or famous people.

1 Bend the arms of the hanger, as shown.

2 Slide the bent arms into the tube. Push the tube up to the neck of the hanger.

3 Draw a picture of a famous person and cut it out. (The cutout should be no more than 9–10 inches in height.)

4 Glue the cutout to the cardboard tube.

5 Research and then write about the person on an index card.

6 Slide the card between the arms of the hanger and position it below the picture cutout, as shown above.

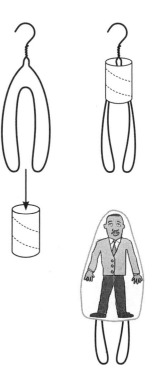

Content Connection: Famous 20th Century Americans

Students select a famous American who made a significant contribution to the country during the 20th century, such as Martin Luther King, Jr., Cesar Chavez, Rachel Carson, or Rosa Parks. (If desired, provide a list of people for students to choose from.) Students then do research to find images of their person and learn about their life and contributions. Using what they have learned, students complete a biography hanger frame for their subject. When finished, they share their work with the class. Finally, students display their frames in the classroom (see Tips).

40 Fabulous Social Studies Activities © 2013 by Catherine M. Tamblyn, Scholastic Teaching Resources

Birthday Marker Hangers

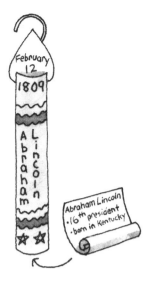

These birthday marker hangers offer students a flexible method for highlighting and sequencing important historical figures by their birthdate.

Materials

For each student:

- paper towel tube
- markers
- wire shirt hanger
- $2\frac{1}{2}$-inch square of yellow paper
- scissors
- half-sheet of copy paper
- clothesline

Tips

- Students might create hangers to represent dates other than birthdays. (Leave off the candle flame.)

- To make dividers, label the tubes with different time divisions, such as months or years (no flame needed).

Other Content Connections

- inventors
- famous Americans
- statehood dates

1 Select a historical figure and write that person's birth year near the top of the tube. Add the person's name and decorate the tube.

2 Cut a candle flame from the yellow square. Label it with the month and day of the person's birth.

3 Bend the arms of the hanger, as shown.

4 Slide the bent arms into the tube. Push the tube up to the neck of the hanger.

5 Cut two slits opposite each other in the top of the tube. Insert the flame into the slits.

6 Write facts about the person on the half-sheet of paper. Roll the paper (like a scroll) and insert it into the bottom of the tube.

7 Hang the birthday marker hanger on a clothesline.

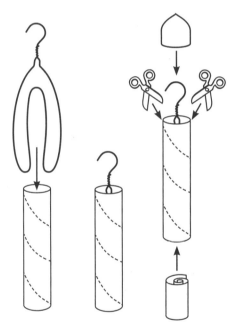

Content Connections: Procession of Presidents

Students create a birthday marker hanger for a U.S. president of their choice. (You might list the presidents on chart paper and have each student choose a different one.) When finished, students sequence their hangers on a clothesline by the birthdates of the presidents. Or you can adapt this activity to line up presidents in order of their terms of service. To use, students choose a tube and remove the rolled paper to learn more about that president.

Trading Cards

M aking trading cards that feature accomplished sports figures, famous Americans, or important world leaders provides students with a creative way to share their research and interesting facts.

For each student:

- trading card pattern (page 31)
- crayons, markers, or colored pencils
- scissors
- glue stick

Tip

Copy the trading card pattern onto a different color of paper for each group of people to be represented. (Use light colors.) For example, you might use blue for U.S. Presidents, yellow for sports figures, green for inventors, and so on.

Other Content Connections

- historical and contemporary figures
- well-known explorers
- inventors and innovators

1 Cut out the card and fold it in half along the long, solid line.

2 Glue the top, bottom, and right edges together to create a two-sided card.

3 Fill out the information on the trading card about a selected person. Add drawings where indicated.

Content Connection: Favorite Athletes

Students make a trading card. Then they complete information about their favorite athlete on the card. First, they fill in the athlete's name, draw his or her picture, and write the athlete's occupation (sport and position) on the front. On the back, they list some fun facts about their athlete (such as awards, sports-related records, and birthdate), fill in the athlete's birthplace information, and draw a map showing that location. Finally, they write their name in the box at the bottom. Students can then share their cards with the class and use a map to locate the birthplace of their athlete.

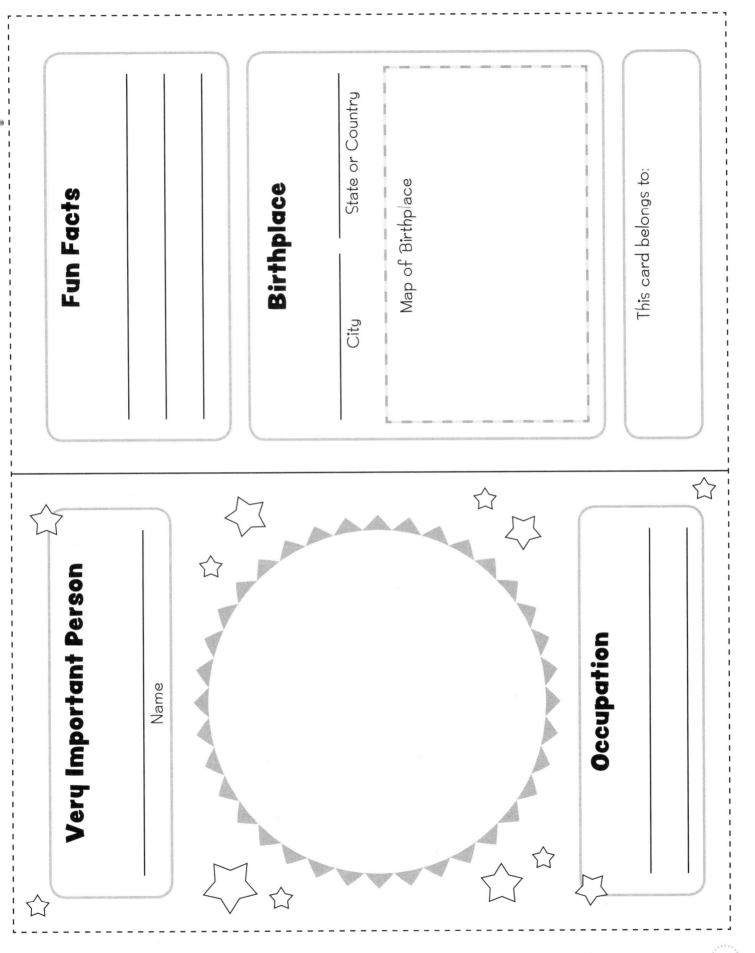

Fun Facts

Birthplace

City

State or Country

Map of Birthplace

This card belongs to:

Very Important Person

Name

Occupation

Cut-Away Books

Cut-away books have covers that are shaped like a famous person's profile, a historical building, or any imaginative form students might choose.

1 For the cover, fold a sheet of paper in half the short way.

2 Choose a person to research. Draw that person's profile on the folded paper (with fold to left). Fill up as much space as possible.

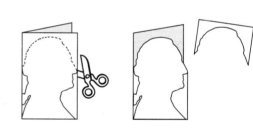

3 Cut out the upper third of the profile through the top layer only. Trim away the excess along the fold. (Do not cut along the rest of the fold.)

4 Fold several additional sheets of paper in half the short way. Staple the pages inside the cover along the left edge.

5 Add a title and author line to the cover. If desired, color the background around the lower part of the profile. Add art and information about the person to complete the interior pages.

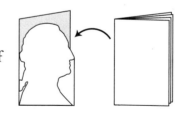

Content Connection: Presidential Profiles

Provide students with copies of the president profiles on page 33. Students choose one of the profiles (Washington or Lincoln), cut it out, and glue it near the top of the folded paper (see step 1 in directions). Then they make a cut-away book as described in steps 3 through 5. On the interior pages, students can write facts or a story about their president and add art to go with their text.

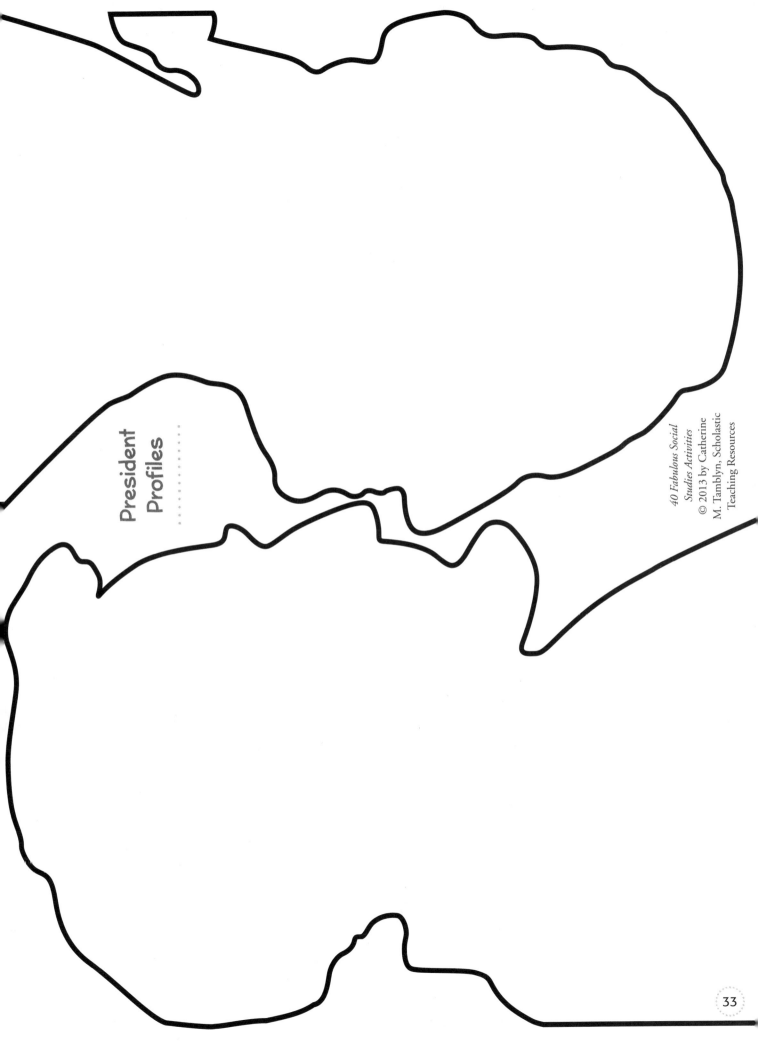

President Profiles
. . . .

Wrap-Around Monuments

These wrap-around monuments provide students a fun format in which to share facts about and pay tribute to historical or famous people.

Materials

For each student:

- monument pattern (page 35)
- scissors
- crayons, markers, or colored pencils
- 1- or 2-liter plastic soda bottle (clean, with label removed)
- tape

Tips

- If desired, students can use craft items to embellish their monuments (such as yarn for hair, buttons for eyes, and fabric for clothing).
- To help keep the bottle from tipping over, add sand and put a lid on the bottle.

Other Content Connections

- famous African Americans, Hispanic Americans, or Native Americans
- national or local heroes
- community workers

1 Cut out the monument pattern. Choose a person to research. Decorate the top part of the cutout to resemble that person.

2 Fill in the person's name in the small box. Write about the person in the large box.

3 Wrap the cutout around the bottle and secure with tape.

Content Connections: Monuments to Women

Students create a wrap-around monument to honor a special woman and her achievements or contributions to society. (This project works well for Women's History Month). If desired, make a list of historical or famous women for students to choose from. Or provide a collection of books about famous women for students to browse through to make their choice. Display the completed monuments on a table, windowsill, bookshelf, or other flat surface. Students can then visit the monuments to learn about different women and the important roles they played in our world.

40 Fabulous Social Studies Activities © 2013 by Catherine M. Tamblyn, Scholastic Teaching Resources

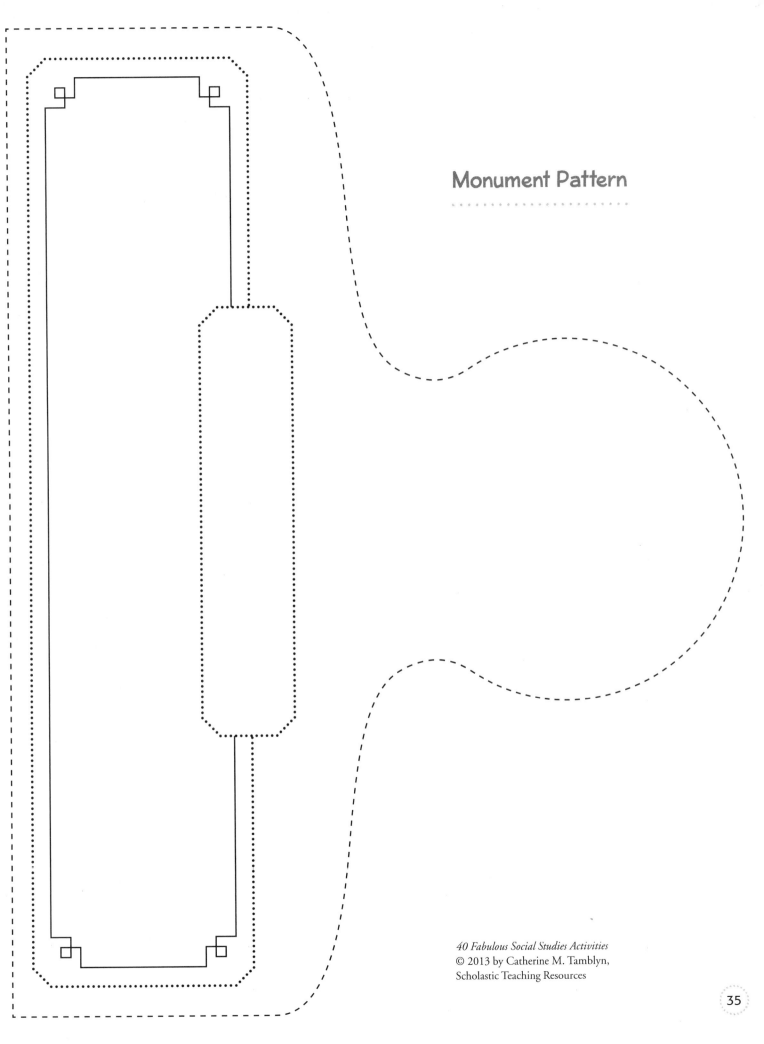

Monument Pattern

40 Fabulous Social Studies Activities
© 2013 by Catherine M. Tamblyn,
Scholastic Teaching Resources

Portrait Plates

Portrait plates offer students the opportunity to create likenesses of historical people, notable contemporary figures, self-portraits, and more.

Tip

Instead of drawing their famous person, students might use copies of the person's image obtained from books or the Internet.

Other Content Connections

- notable historical or contemporary figures
- community workers and jobs
- self-portraits and facts about self

1 Choose a famous person to research. Locate an image of that person.

2 Draw a picture of the person on the plate. If desired, use craft supplies for the person's features, such as the eyes, hair, and personal accessories.

3 Write facts about the person on the index card. Glue the card to the back of the plate.

4 Tape a craft-stick handle to the back.

Content Connection: People From the Past

Label index cards with the names of people from the past and distribute to students. To begin, students do research to find images of their person and gather facts. Using their results, students then create a portrait plate featuring that person. When finished, students can use their projects to share information about their person with the class. Or, they might give clues for the class to use to guess their person's identity.

Simple Shutter Books

These quick-and-easy books, featuring two shutters (or flaps) that open to reveal hidden information, offer students a simple way to present information on a variety of topics.

Materials

For each student:
- 8½ - by 14-inch sheet of paper

Tip

To make a stand for the book, cut two one-inch slits opposite each other in a 1½-inch tall cardboard tube. Slide the bottom of the shutter book into the slits, leaving the shutters free to open and close. Stand the book on a flat surface.

1 Fold the paper in half the short way and crease lightly. Unfold the paper.

2 Fold each short side toward the center and crease at the fold. The two sides form the "shutters" of the book.

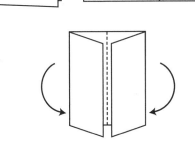

3 Choose a topic to research. Label the shutters with a title for the topic. Add illustrations, if desired.

4 Open the shutters. Write about the topic on the inside of the book, including the shutters. Add drawings or picture cutouts, too.

Content Connection: History of Communication

Students choose a topic related to communication, such as telephones, radio, television, or email. They do research to learn about the history of their topic. Then students make a simple shutter book and use their findings to complete it. On the inside, they can provide information about the history of their topic. For example, if their topic is on telephones, they might include information about the different types of phones used over time. When finished, students share their shutter books with the class. Finally, they can display their books on a bulletin board, or make tube stands (see "Tip") and stand the books upright on a flat surface.

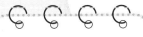

Other Content Connections

- geographical features
- state-specific products and services
- history of inventions

40 Fabulous Social Studies Activities © 2013 by Catherine M. Tamblyn, Scholastic Teaching Resources

Shutter House Books

Shutter house books are in the shape of a house and have two flaps that can be opened and closed. Students can create these houses to feature the home life of families during different times in history.

Materials

For each student:

- house pattern (page 39)
- scissors
- 9- by 12-inch construction paper
- glue stick
- crayons, markers, or colored pencils

Tip

- If desired, students can make a tube stand for displaying their book. (See "Tip" for Simple Shutter Books on page 37.)

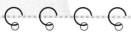

Other Content Connections

- pioneer home or community buildings
- Abraham Lincoln's log cabin
- homes of famous Americans

1 Do research to learn about family life during a particular period of time in history.

2 Cut out the house pattern. Cut the flaps along the broken lines.

3 Fold back each flap. Glue the house to the construction paper, leaving the flaps loose.

4 Trim the construction paper to the outer shape of the house.

5 Decorate the inside and outside of the house with images to represent the time period. Write text on the inside of the flaps.

Content Connection: Pilgrim Life

Students do research to learn about Pilgrim life during colonial times. Then they create a shutter house book to represent a Pilgrim home. First, students draw a clapboard design on the front of the house and decorate the roof to resemble a thatched roof. Next, they open the flaps and draw a scene depicting the interior of a Pilgrim home. Finally, students write about Pilgrim life on the inside of the flaps.

Mix-and-Match Flipbooks

Materials

For each student:

- 6- by 18-inch piece of cardboard
- 3- by 5-inch plain index cards
- hole punch
- ruler
- crayons, markers, or colored pencils
- 3 metal rings

With these versatile flipbooks, students check their knowledge of historical events or people by matching pages that contain related facts about the same topic.

1 Make three stacks of index cards. Use the same number of cards in each stack. Punch a hole at the center of one long edge in each stack.

2 Arrange the three stacks one inch apart near a long edge of the cardboard. (The left and right stacks will be about $\frac{1}{2}$ inch from the short edges.)

3 Mark through the holes in the cards to show their placement on the cardboard. Remove the cards and punch a hole through the cardboard at each mark.

4 Label each stack of cards with the desired information. Add drawings, if desired. Mix up the order of cards in each stack.

5 Use metal rings to attach each stack to the cardboard.

Content Connection: Inventors

Students do research to learn about inventors and their inventions. Then they make a mix-and-match flipbook in which to record their findings. Students label the stack of cards on the left with the name of their inventors, the middle cards with verbs describing what the inventors did (such as "invented," "created," or "prepared"), and the cards on the right with the inventions. They can add drawings, if desired. They might also add sticky notes labeled "Who," "did," and "what?" below the three stacks of pages. To use, students flip the pages to find the three pages that make a true statement.

Tips

- For self-checking purposes, students can label the back of the cards that go together (in the first, middle, and last stacks) with a matching number, symbol, or color.
- If desired, attach sticky notes along the bottom of the cardboard flipbook backing to label each stack of cards. (See above.)

Other Content Connections

- U.S. Founding Fathers
- government branches and duties
- national sites and monuments (locations, descriptions)

Facts-on-Flaps Booklets

The facts-on-flaps booklet format gives students a unique way to organize and record facts about famous people or historical events, create timelines, or compare events, figures, or places.

1 Stack and fold two sheets of paper into thirds the short way. Lightly crease the folds, then unfold.

2 Stack the creased pages onto another sheet of paper. Fold that stack in half the long way. Staple along the folded edge.

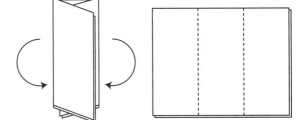

3 Cut along the fold lines of the interior pages to make three sets of flaps. (Do not cut through the front and back cover.)

4 Turn the booklet horizontally with the fold at the top. Title and decorate the front cover.

5 Label the top flap of each section with a topic, then write facts about that topic on the other flaps in that section. Use the front and back of the flaps, if desired.

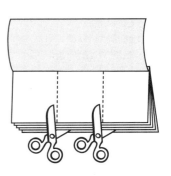

Content Connection: Early Explorers

Students do research to learn about three early explorers, such as those who sailed to America. Then they create a flap booklet. On the inside, students label the top flap of each section with the name and picture of one of their explorers. They write a fact about that explorer on each flap in the section and add a drawing, if desired. Finally, students use the booklets to share about their explorers with the class.

Supersize Stamps

Cruise Ship

Students create these larger-than-life stamps to feature historic figures, places, events, and other images that depict traditions and culture of American life.

Materials

For each student:

- stamp pattern (page 44)
- markers
- scissors
- glue stick
- 9- by 12-inch sheet of construction paper

Other Content Connections

- inventors and inventions
- history of communication
- state trees, birds, flags

1 Choose a topic and draw a related picture on the stamp, vertically or horizontally. If desired, add "U.S.A." in a corner to give the stamp a more authentic look.

Note: If planning to create coils or stamp books (see page 43), stamps should all be designed either horizontally or vertically.

2 Cut out the stamp.

3 Glue the stamp to construction paper. Write about the topic on the back of the page.

Content Connection: History of Transportation

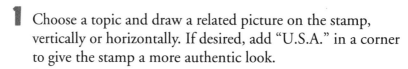

Students make a supersize stamp related to the history of transportation. Before they begin, assign a specific mode of land, water, or air transportation to each individual to research. Or, assign to students people who have made significant contributions to transportation, such as Amelia Earhart, Henry Ford, Robert Fulton, Mae Jemison, Eduardo San Juan, and Orville and Wilbur Wright. After students complete their stamps, they write about their topic on the back to tell about its history and importance in moving people and goods, or in advancing knowledge or technology. Finally, display the stamps individually, or prepare large "coils" or a book with students' stamps. (See page 43.)

40 Fabulous Social Studies Activities © 2013 by Catherine M. Tamblyn, Scholastic Teaching Resources

Make a Coil of Supersize Stamps

Creating a coil of stamps provides an interesting way for students to display and use their stamps. To make a coil, students place two stamps facedown side by side and use masking tape to tape them together along the back edges. Students add one stamp at a time in this manner to create a long row. If desired, they can organize the stamps by topic, time period, common characteristics, or other grouping criteria. Or, they can make separate coils for each group. When finished, students roll the connected stamps into a coil. To use, students uncoil the stamps to find their own, then share the information on it with the class. Display by unrolling the coil and hanging the strip of stamps on a clothesline.

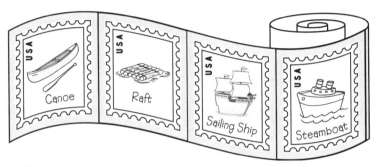

Make a Book of Supersize Stamps

For another display option, arrange the stamps into "stamp books." Provide an 18- by 72-inch strip of bulletin board paper for every twelve stamps. To make a stamp book, students fold the paper strip into thirds. Then they use double-sided, removable tape to attach four stamps faceup to each section of the strip. Students can remove their stamp from the book to share it with the class, then return it when finished. To display, unfold the book and hang it on a classroom wall or door.

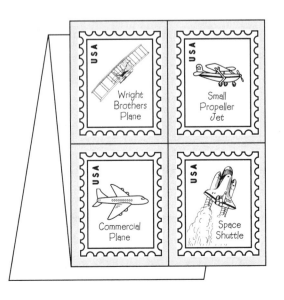

Stamp Pattern

Codex Books

Students can make these pocket-size codex books to record facts, timelines, and stories about any number of topics.

Materials

For each student:
- $8\frac{1}{2}$- by 11-inch copy paper
- scissors
- glue stick
- two 5- by 6-inch pieces of tagboard
- hole punch
- 16-inch length of yarn

Tips

- For more sturdy covers, use cardboard instead of tagboard.
- To make a longer codex book, use an additional sheet of paper. (Each sheet will add four more panels to the book.)

Other Content Connections

- Pilgrims (voyage and settlement)
- timeline of historical U.S. expeditions
- sequence in a manufacturing process

1 Fold two sheets of paper in half the long way. Cut along the fold through both layers to make four strips of paper.

2 Glue the strips together end to end to create one long strip.

3 Accordion-fold the long strip into eight equal panels.

4 Glue tagboard to the top and bottom panels to create a front and back cover.

5 Unfold the book. Write about a selected topic on each panel and add drawings. Then refold the book.

6 Punch a hole near the right edge of each cover. Tie the yarn to the hole in the back cover.

7 Thread the yarn through the hole in the front cover and tie.

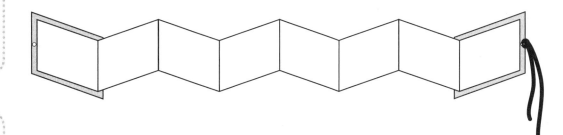

Content Connection: Life on the Oregon Trail

Students do research to learn about life on the Oregon Trail during the westward movement of the mid-1800s. Topics they might learn about include covered wagons, pioneer family life, wagon trains and circles, hardships on the trail, geographic features along the Oregon Trail, and so on. Students then use their findings to create a codex book. They can share their completed book with partners or small groups.

Trifold Table Toppers

With three simple folds, students can create these self-standing table toppers to feature facts about a historical place, important inventor, or famous person.

Castillo de San Marcos
This is a fort that was built by the Spanish in 1672-1695. It guarded St. Augustine, Florida, which was the first permanent European settlement in the United States. The fort was made a National Monument in 1924. It became part of the National Park System in 1933.

Materials

For each student:
- 9- by 12-inch sheet of construction paper
- ruler
- scissors
- tape

• Tips •

- Fold the paper the long way to make a shorter, wider table topper.
- Use various paper sizes to create table toppers of different widths and heights.

Other Content Connections

- artifacts and their history or use
- inventions and inventors
- workers, services, and goods

1 Fold the paper in half the short way.

2 Cut a $\frac{1}{2}$-inch slit in the middle of the sides opposite the fold. Cut through both layers.

3 Fold in each slitted side $1\frac{1}{2}$ inches toward the center.

4 Turn the paper so that the fold is at the top. Write about a selected topic and add drawings to one side, then the other.

5 Unfold the page just enough to slide the two slits into each other, creating a tent with a base. Tape to secure.

6 Stand the table topper upright on a flat surface.

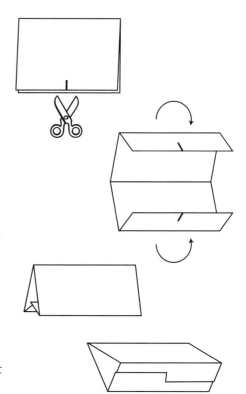

Content Connection: Historic Places

Students select a historic place, such as a colonial community, fort, or mission to research. They use their findings to create a trifold table topper. Students might add text and drawings to both sides of their topper, or place text on one side and illustrations on the other. When finished, students present their projects to the class, then stand them on a flat surface to display. If desired, group the table toppers by topic, time periods, or location.

Portable Partitions

These colorful, "walk-around" partitions help give a museum-like appearance to class displays while providing a perfect way to expand display space for students' work.

1 Cut off the box flaps. Or tape them securely to the inside of the box.

2 Work with a small group to paint a panel of the box. (Each group will be assigned a different color and a different side or the bottom of the box to paint.)

3 Allow the paint on each side to dry.

4 Stand the box upside down (open end down). The bottom of the box will be the top of the partition.

5 Tape or staple class work and projects to the sides of the partition.

Content Connection: Transportation Then and Now

Prepare a large box to be decorated for use as a portable partition. Students then work together in small groups to paint the box. After the partition is set up in the classroom, students use double-sided removable tape to attach the supersize stamps they made in History of Transportation (page 42). Add a title to the display. Or use a sheet of 12- by 18-inch construction paper to make a table topper (see Trifold Table Toppers, page 46) labeled with the display title, then place on the top of the partition.

Banner Hang-Ups

Citizens in Action

Wear a helmet.

Students can create and display these quick-and-easy banners to advertise what they have learned about citizenship, the environment, government, or any other topic.

Materials

For each student, pair, or small group:

- mural paper
- cardboard gift-wrap tube
- scissors
- tape
- markers
- yarn

Tips

- Students can craft small banners from construction paper attached to paper towel tubes or drinking straws.

- To prevent curling, glue a one-inch wide strip of tagboard or cardboard along the back edge of each side and bottom of the banner.

Other Content Connections

- environmental awareness (recycling, wise use of energy and resources)

- community volunteering (helping others, working together)

- citizen's rights and responsibilities

1 Trim the width of the mural paper to fit the length of a tube.

2 Wrap the top edge of the paper around the tube and tape it to the back of the paper. (This will create a sleeve for the tube.)

3 Cut the paper to the desired length.

4 Decorate the front of the banner.

5 To make a hanger, cut a length of yarn about three times the length of the tube. Thread the yarn through the tube and tie the ends together.

Content Connection: Citizens in Action

Students work in pairs or small groups to create a banner hang-up about being an active citizen. To begin, each group decides on its topic, such as safety rules to follow at school or in the community. Students then work together to plan and decorate their banner. They can draw their own illustrations or use cutouts from magazines, catalogs, or images printed from the Internet. After groups present their banners to the class, students can hang them on a bulletin board or in other areas of the room.

Class Scrolls

These class scrolls provide students with a large workspace on which they can communicate ideas and feature art related to a number of different topics.

Materials

For one scroll:
- 5½ foot length of mural paper
- 2 cardboard gift-wrap tubes
- glue
- pipe cleaner or 12-inch length of ribbon

Tips

- If the gift-wrap tube is taller than the paper, trim to fit.
- Students can make small, individual scrolls using paper towel tubes and several 11- by 17-inch sheets of copy paper taped together.

Other Content Connections

- community, state, or national laws
- citizens' rights and responsibilities
- branches of government

1 Choose a topic, then decorate the length of the mural paper with text and art to represent that topic. (Leave about six inches on each short side of the paper blank.)

2 Glue each short edge of the paper to a cardboard tube.

3 Roll each tube toward the center of the paper to make a scroll.

4 Wrap a pipe cleaner around the scroll to secure, or tie a length of ribbon around it.

Content Connection: Classroom Constitution

Work with students to generate a list of class rules that help promote a safe and peaceful environment. The list might include rules about being fair, showing respect, sharing, using manners, being a good listener, and cooperating with others. Afterward, students vote to determine the top five rules on the list. Then they gather into five groups and choose one of the five rules. Next, each group labels and decorates a one-foot section of the scroll to represent its rule and students sign their names. (Title the top of the scroll "Our Class Constitution" in advance.) To complete, assemble the scroll, roll and secure, then set it in a special place. Then, to begin each day, volunteers can unroll the scroll, read the rules aloud, and attach it to a display to serve as a reminder of the rules throughout the day.

Poster-Board Shields

S tudents can make these poster-board shields and decorate them with mottos, geometric motifs, flags, or other symbols to represent their topic of study.

Materials

For each student:
- poster board (or 18- by 24-inch sheet of cardboard)
- scissors
- crayons, markers, or colored pencils
- 1- by 10-inch strip of tagboard
- wide clear tape

Tip

Students can use different shapes for their shields, such as the typical badge-like shape, an oval, circle, rectangle, or diamond.

Other Content Connections

- family coat-of arms
- patriotic themes (such as "Freedom is _____.")
- multicultural celebrations (e.g., Black History Month, Hispanic History Month)

1 Research a chosen topic. Plan a shield design to represent that topic.

2 Draw the shape of a shield on the poster board. Make the shape as large as possible.

3 Cut out the shield and decorate it.

4 For the handle, fold back a 1-inch tab on each end of the tagboard strip. Tape the handle, tabs down, to the center back of the shield.

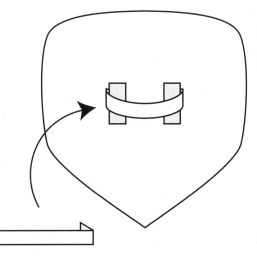

Content Connection: American Symbols

Work with students to generate a list of American symbols, including the American flag, Liberty Bell, Statue of Liberty, Uncle Sam, White House, and bald eagle. If desired, add other symbols, such as those for the Republican and Democratic parties (elephant and donkey), the Pledge of Allegiance, U.S. mottos, and the Presidential seal. Students then choose a symbol from the list to research and create a shield using their findings. If desired, students can write about their symbol on the back of their shield. Finally, students present their shields to the class.

40 Fabulous Social Studies Activities © 2013 by Catherine M. Tamblyn, Scholastic Teaching Resources

Theme Quilts

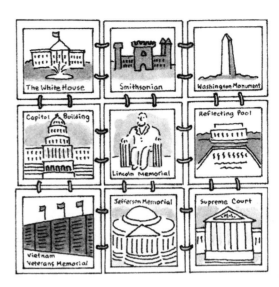

Colonial Americans used quilts for decoration, bedding, and other practical purposes. With this project, students make "quilt squares" to represent a particular theme or topic.

Materials

For a class quilt:

- 8-inch squares of copy paper
- crayons, markers, or colored pencils
- 9-inch construction paper squares
- glue stick
- ruler
- hole punch
- yarn
- scissors

Tips

- If needed, use plain construction paper "quilt squares" to fill in the quilt grid.
- Students whose quilt squares will form the top, bottom, or side edges of the class quilt can opt not to punch holes in those sides of their squares.

Other Content Connections

- U.S. or state symbols
- U. S. presidents
- timeline of historical events

1 Choose a topic from a theme to learn about. Draw a picture to represent the topic on a copy-paper square. (Label it, if desired.)

2 Glue the picture to a square of construction paper. This will become a "quilt square."

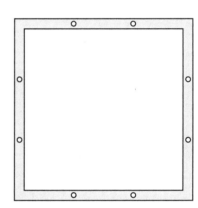

3 Using a ruler and pencil, make a dot at the 3- and 6-inch marks on each side of the quilt square. (For squares along the top, bottom, and sides edges, see "Tips.")

4 Arrange the quilt square with those made by other classmates to form a large grid.

5 Work with classmates to "sew" the quilt squares together by lacing yarn through the holes. (See picture above.)

Content Connection: Our National Capital

Provide students with red, white, and blue construction paper squares and yarn. If desired, assign construction paper colors to student so that the pages can be arranged in an alternating pattern to form the quilt. To begin, students choose a historical building, monument, or other site in Washington, D.C. to research and learn about. Then they use their findings to create a "quilt square." Afterward, students assemble a whole-class quilt or several small-group quilts with their squares. When completed, students can point out their quilt square and tell the class about the structure featured on it.

Folding Fans

Hand-held fans have often been used in ceremonies and dances, for cooling oneself, as toys, and much more. Students can make these unique folding fans to represent a topic they have learned about.

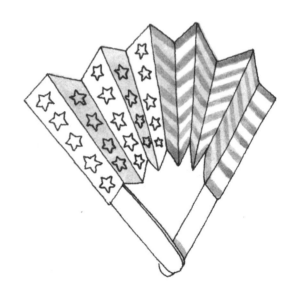

Materials

For each student:
- 5½ - by 12-inch sheet of construction paper
- crayons, markers, or colored pencils
- two wide craft sticks
- glue
- self-adhesive Velcro® dots

Tip

Students might use a craft punch to make a decorative hole-punch design along the top edge of their fan.

1 Place the construction paper horizontally. Draw a picture to represent a selected topic.

2 Accordion-fold the paper from left to right. Fold it back and forth ten times to make 11 sections. (Each section will be about one inch wide.)

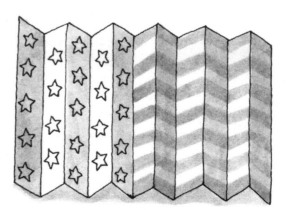

3 Turn the paper over and unfold. Write facts or information about your design on the sections. (Do not write on the two end sections.)

4 Glue a craft stick to each end section on the back, leaving about $3\frac{1}{2}$ inches extending beyond the bottom edge.

5 With the fan still facedown, attach a Velcro hook or loop dot to the bottom of each craft stick. Place one dot on the back of the left stick and the other on the front of the right stick.

6 Turn the fan faceup. Angle the sticks outward to spread out the fan. Press the Velcro dots together to secure.

7 To close, fold the fan together, stacking the sticks one on top of the other, and press at the dots to secure.

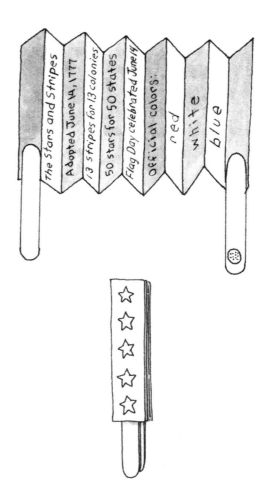

Content Connection: The American Flag

Students do research to learn about the history, designs, and traditions of the U.S. flag. Then they decorate one side of the $5\frac{1}{2}$-inch by 12-inch sheet of construction paper with a flag design. After students accordion-fold the page, they write facts or other interesting information about their flag on the back sections. For instance, they might write about the flag colors, the symbolism of the 13 stripes and 50 stars, Flag Day facts, and so on. As an alternative, students can copy or write a short poem or haiku about the flag. After assembling their fan, students share them with classmates.

Other Content Connections

- national parks or historic sites
- national holidays
- Earth Day symbols and concepts

One-Cut Pennants

These simple one-cut pennants allow student pairs to showcase their knowledge about a variety of topics in an eye-catching, sporty-looking display.

Fish

Trees

Materials

For each student pair:

- 14- by 48-inch sheet of mural paper
- scissors
- markers, crayons, or colored pencils
- wire or plastic shirt hanger
- glue stick or tape

Tips

- Pennants can be made in a variety of sizes, shapes, or lengths and the single cut can be curved, zigzag, wavy, and so on. (See page 55.)
- Instead of using hangers or yarn, students might use clothespins to suspend their pennants from a clothesline.

Make a Shirt-Hanger Pennant

1 Work with a partner to do research on the chosen topic. Together, draw a V-shape in the middle of the mural paper, as shown.

2 Cut the paper in two along the line to make two pennants (one for each partner).

3 Decorate and label each pennant to represent the topic of choice. If desired, write about the topic on the back.

4 Make a one-inch fold along the top short edge of the pennants.

5 Fit the fold over the bottom of the hanger. Glue or tape in place.

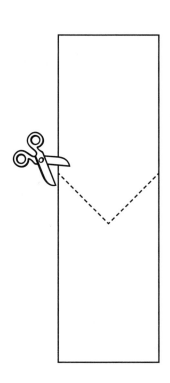

Make a Yarn Hanger Pennant

To make a pennant with a yarn hanger, follow steps 1–4 in the directions. Then glue the folded edge of the pennant over a length of yarn, being careful not to trap the yarn in the glue. Finally, tie the ends of the yarn together.

One-Cut Options for Banners

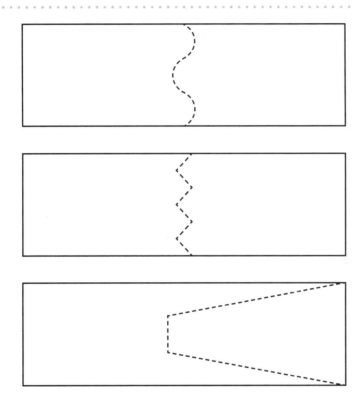

Content Connection: Natural Resources

Student pairs do research to learn about a local, state, or national natural resource. Then the partners make banners to represent their natural resource. They can draw a picture of the resource, how it is used, or a product made from it. Then students label their illustration and turn over the pennants to add facts or other information about their resource on the back. As a variation, students might illustrate and write about one or more ways to respect and care for their resource.

Other Content Connections

- endangered animals or habitats
- alternative energy sources
- local or state goods (milk, lumber, paper)

40 Fabulous Social Studies Activities © 2013 by Catherine M. Tamblyn, Scholastic Teaching Resources

3-D Flow Charts

For these 3-D flow charts, students create a paper-plate cube that depicts a particular process, such as harvesting trees, assembling a product, or moving goods from manufacturing to market.

Materials

For each student:

- six 6-inch paper plates
- crayons, markers, or colored pencils
- stapler

Tip

Students might use 9-inch paper plates if they need a larger space on which to write about and draw the steps of their process.

Other Content Connections

- paper-making process
- production of dairy products
- processing recyclables

1 Choose a process to research. Break the process down into five steps.

2 Write the title of the process on one paper plate and add a drawing.

3 On each additional plate, write about a step in the process. Number each step (from 1–5) and include a drawing.

4 Staple the title plate to the plate with step 1 along the rims.

5 Staple the other plates together to form a cube that shows the sequence of the process. (Connect each plate to the plates labeled with the steps that come before and after that step.)

6 Draw an arrow on each plate that points to the step that follows. (For example, point the arrow on the title plate to the step 1 plate, the step 1 plate to the step 2 plate, and so on.)

Content Connection: How Trees Are Harvested

Students do research to learn about how trees are harvested and prepared for use as a marketable product, such as lumber. When finished, they outline the process into five steps to use on their 3-D flow chart. For example, the steps for harvesting tress from forest to mill might include: 1. Growers plant and tend the trees; 2. Foresters choose the trees to cut; 3. Fallers saw the trees; 4. Transporters move the logs to sawmills; and 5. Millers remove the bark, cut the logs, and saw them into lumber. Students can add their own drawings to each step or glue on picture cutouts printed from the Internet. When completed, students use their 3-D flow charts to describe their process to the class.

Recyclables Frames

Materials

For each student:

- recyclable materials (see Tips, below)
- scissors
- craft glue
- stapler
- tape
- crayons, markers, or colored pencils
- craft items (scrap paper, yarn, ribbon, buttons, and so on)

These frames, made from recyclable materials, give students the opportunity to put into practice the concept of repurposing a variety of items.

Ocean dumping harms whales and other sea animals.

Tips

- Recyclable items that work well for the frame base include foam trays, plastic containers, large plastic lids, cardboard, and egg cartons.
- Attachments to the frames might be made from recyclable items, such as cardboard tubes, foil, plastic wrap, foam peanuts, plastic bottle caps, magazine cutouts, and broken trinkets.

1 Choose a recyclable item to use as the frame base. (See Tips.)

2 If needed, trim a sheet of construction paper to fit the bottom of the base. Glue the paper in place.

3 Plan a design, picture, or concept to represent in the frame. If desired, sketch out the idea on the base.

4 Complete the design by drawing and coloring illustrations or adding craft items to give it a 3-D effect. (See Tips.) Glue, staple, or tape the recyclable materials in place.

Content Connection: Earth Day

Students choose an environmental theme or eco-friendly action to highlight—for instance, saving energy, conserving water, reducing waste, hazards of ocean dumping, or protecting endangered species and habitats. They then create a recyclables frame to represent their theme. If using loose articles inside a base that has depth, such as a takeout tray, students can use clear plastic wrap to enclose the articles. Finally, they describe the concept represented by their frame by writing about it on a recyclable paper product (such as a scrap of paper or cardboard tube) and attaching it to the project.

Other Content Connections

- Arbor Day
- noted environmental activists
- "green" occupations

Accordion Shape Books

Accordion shape books give students a unique way to feature facts and information using shapes that fit the theme or concept of their selected topic.

Materials

For each student:

- $5\frac{1}{2}$- by 17-inch strip of paper
- pencil
- scissors
- crayons, markers, or colored pencils

Tips

- Cut 11- by 17-inch sheets of paper in half lengthwise to make the strips of paper.
- Instead of drawing a shape, students might glue on a shape cutout and cut around it, leaving the folds intact as part of the sides of the shape.

Other Content Connections

- national leaders or heroes
- timeline of historical events or holidays
- national, state, or local industries or products

1 Fold the paper strip in half two times. Unfold the paper.

2 Refold the paper back and forth accordion-style to make a book with four sections.

3 Draw a large shape on the top section to represent the selected theme or concept. Fill up as much of the space as possible, checking that the sides of the shape touch the folds on both sides.

4 Cut around the top and bottom of the shape through all layers. Do not cut away the sides that touch the folds.

5 Unfold the book. For the cover, add a title, author line, and art to the section on the left.

6 Complete each section (or page) with text and an illustration. Turn the book over and complete each back page. Then fold the book so that the cover is on top.

Content Connection: Community Badges of Honor

Work with students to make a list of official and nonofficial community leaders, such as mayor, judge, fire chief, sheriff, librarian, scout groups, and volunteers. Afterward, students can cut out a copy of the badge pattern (page 59) and use it to make the shape for their accordion shape book. They simply glue the cutout to the top section of their folded book and cut around the top and bottom through all layers, leaving the folds intact at the sides. Then students complete their book, featuring a different community leader on each page.

Badge Pattern

Community
Badges
of Honor

by _____

Community
Badges
of Honor

by _____

Stage Triforms

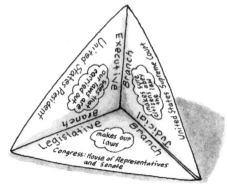

These free-standing stage triforms offer students three sides on which to make comparisons, feature historical people and places, depict changes over periods of time, or highlight facts about important events.

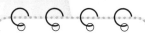

1 Fold the square diagonally, then unfold.

2 Repeat step 1, folding the paper diagonally from the other two corners.

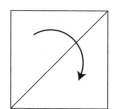 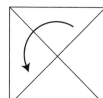

3 Starting at any corner, cut along one fold to the center of the paper. Mark an X on one section next to the cut. (This section will not be drawn or written on.)

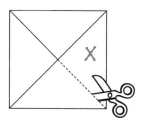

4 Write about the selected topic on each unmarked section. Add art, if desired.

5 Overlap the decorated cut section over the marked X. Glue in place.

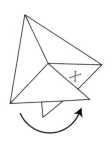

6 To display, stand the triform on a flat surface.

Content Connection: Branches of Government

Students research the three branches of the United States government (executive, legislative, and judicial). Then they create a stage triform, completing each side with facts and information about one of the three branches. Students can add art, such as a drawing or a cutout of the Presidential Seal, United States Capitol, and Supreme Court Building to enhance their project. When finished, students use their triforms to present their findings to the class.

Quadruple Triforms

Quadruple triforms—four-sided versions of the stage triforms (page 60)—give students more space to feature facts, sequence historical events, chronicle the evolution of inventions, and much more.

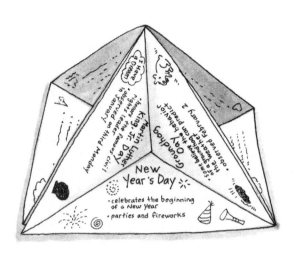

Materials

For each student:

- four 8-inch paper squares
- scissors
- markers or colored pencils
- glue stick
- stapler (optional)

Tip

If desired, students can decorate only the upright sides of their triforms, then add 3-D features by attaching self-standing picture cutouts or small objects on the "floor" of each one.

Other Content Connections

- evolution of an invention (car, computer, airplane)
- timeline of historical events
- steps in product development

1 Follow the directions on page 60 to make a stage triform with each paper square.

2 Glue (or staple) the outer sides of two triforms together. Repeat with the other two triforms.

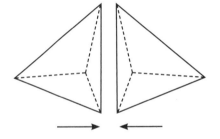

3 Glue (or staple) the pairs of triforms together back to back to make a four-sided triform. If needed, arrange and glue together the triforms to sequence events or information in a logical order.

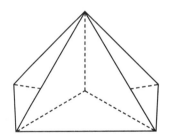

Content Connection: Special Celebrations

Work with the class to generate a list of national and cultural celebrations. Afterward, students choose celebrations from the list to feature on a quadruple triform. They might write about and illustrate a different celebration on each of the twelve interior sides of their triform. Or, they can feature a different celebration on each triform. When completed, students share their triforms with a small group or the whole class.

Zip Books

Zip books make it possible for students to include actual objects, artifacts, artwork, and photos in their book without altering those materials.

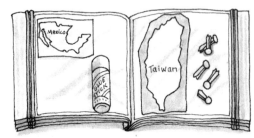

1 Stack the number of bags needed for the book pages. The top bag will serve as the front cover and the first page. Each additional bag can be used for two pages (front and back).

2 Staple along the bottom edge of the bags.

3 Edge the stapled end of the book with masking tape to cover the staples.

4 Label and illustrate both sides of a bag-size sheet of paper to represent the desired topic or concept. (Each side will serve as a separate page.)

5 Insert each sheet of paper into a bag. Add any related articles to the corresponding side of the bag, then seal tightly.

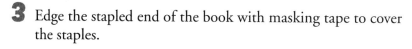

Content Connection: Where Does It Come From?

Students check the product labels on items such as clothing, food, toys, and school supplies to discover their country of origin. (Or they can browse catalogs and cut out pictures of objects made in different countries.) After students construct a zip book, they prepare the cover and label each front or back page with the name of an item, the country in which it was produced, and a map of that country. Then they place the actual item, or a picture, into the corresponding side of the bag. To extend the learning, students can use a large world map or globe to locate the countries mentioned in their books.

Folding Postcards

These easy-to-make postcards allow students to illustrate and describe people, places, or events, as well as write brief messages related to any social studies topics.

Materials

For each student:

- postcard pattern (page 64)
- scissors
- glue stick
- crayons, markers, or colored pencils
- pencil

Tips

- If desired, skip step 2 to create postcards that students can stand on a flat surface to display.
- Students can use the postcard pattern to prepare class invitations for special events, announcements, or thank-you notes.

Other Content Connections

- states or countries
- national or historic places (Washington, D.C. landmarks)
- American symbols

1 Cut out the postcard pattern and fold it in half along the solid line.

2 Glue the back of the folded sides together.

3 Draw a picture related to the selected topic on the front (blank side) of the postcard.

4 On the back, write a caption for the picture in the box on the left.

5 Write a message about the topic below the box.

6 Address the right side of the postcard. Draw a stamp design in the box at the top.

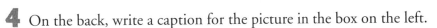

Content Connection: Thank You, Workers

Students discuss the service of community or school workers and volunteers, such as crossing guards, police officers, firefighters, letter carriers, street department workers, bus drivers, classroom volunteers, coaches, and school personnel. Then they prepare a postcard to express their appreciation to a school worker or volunteer that they know or who has been helpful to them.

Postcard Pattern

40 Fabulous Social Studies Activities © 2013 by Catherine M. Tamblyn, Scholastic Teaching Resources